Lessons from a Vessel

Zainab Gafur Patel

BookLeaf
Publishing

India | USA | UK

Lessons from a Vessel © 2023 Zainab Gafur Patel

All rights reserved.

No part of this publication may be reproduced, stored in a retrieval system, or transmitted, in any form or by any means, electronic, mechanical, photocopying, recording or otherwise, without the prior written permission of the presenters.

Zainab Gafur Patel asserts the moral right to be identified as author of this work.

Presentation by *BookLeaf Publishing*

Web: www.bookleafpub.com

E-mail: info@bookleafpub.com

ISBN:9789358319507

First edition 2023

DEDICATION

This book is dedicated to all those who battle
with pain - whether through physical or
emotional - on a daily basis. You are not alone.

ACKNOWLEDGEMENT

To my Lord - every client you sent my way
brought their own message of healing.
To my husband for your unwavering gentleness
with me.
To my parents & siblings, for your prayers.
To my beautiful children for cheering me on and
for being patient with me!
To my Aafiyah Family - you know who you are.
And to my incredibly brave and trusting clients.

PREFACE

Even before I knew this was going to be published, I had started my own collection of thoughts about my take on each condition mentioned. From fertility to chronic pain and auto immune illnesses, each client came with their own message. And with each session, I often wondered if i was becoming desensitised but the reality was that my heart stopped aching when I recognised the psychosomatic ways I could help them. Each client has the ability to let go, to think a new pattern, to help themselves. Mental health can be isolating if we think of it as an illness - but if WE work together, the ILLNESS can be replaced with WELLNESS. I really hope I've done my client's justice in bringing understanding and empathy into their worlds.

Vows of Pain

I wake up with you
And sleep with you
The one loyalty I could really do without.

I move differently with you
I sleep differently with you
I wear my clothes in a clumsy way
(left leg leans to support the pain, breath through
it)
Because of your jolting punishment.

I rush a different pattern
Should you punish a little less one day,
It is suddenly a good day and I am 'less lazy'
I eat a little but a lot different

Today it was a superfood
But everyday is a new solution
To the fractures you have caused

I don't need glue for this relationship you have
with me
There are no cracks - you are firm to my
muscles, to my joints
My blood feels raw and punishing

My heart bleeds despair with your steadfastness
I feel
You will not leave me

A union of trauma - my past
Is your present pain.

In Fertility

'Your home is so clean'
'You're so lucky - no sticky fingerprints here.'
'Just the two of you, is it?'

The smile becomes like cracked glass
Fixed and not worth
Repairing

Aimed always at me
Cementing that belief that
I have done something wrong
A defect part somewhere

That validation is found
In my womb
Was incomprehensible
Until that's where I yearned to find it

Isolated in the emotions
Solitary in my defectiveness
At one with the thought of
What is missing?

In my clean sterile home
Where sleep is only disrupted

Because of my thoughts

The miracle stories
Of rainbow babies
And decades later babies

Seem not for me

And meanwhile, test after test
Reason after reason
From nutritionist to womb therapist
Alone in sterile room after sterile room

Like me - the irony

And to see the looks
Or the blithe questions
Do you have children?
Has numbed me
And I am almost grateful for it

Until I am alone,
Touching the empty womb
Where validation hasn't yet come
After the monthly cycle
Touch, test, repeat

'Maybe we could try...'

No more. I stop.

And find, hitting rock bottom
Comfort in the words

'Trust the process.
Let go of
That outcome.'

So I do

And this is where I start.

I Don't Love You - On childhood alienation

Said I
Angry and hateful
Four years old
And so certain that she was right

Everyday I heard
The things you did
And how no one should want to see you
I remember the rooms
Of fake rainbow drawings

Posters saying
'Family Matters.

Six years and now your face
Induces anger in me
So much anger
I kick and scratch
Why won't you stop trying to see me?
I don't need you in my life

Eight and I am scared
You are smiling, a balloon in your hand
Why do you want to see me when I know

I don't want to see you
My wishes, my consent are all important

The rooms are every Saturday
'Family Matters.
A different officer tells
Her that it's not normal
I look at the Playdough
I can't take it home - don't you get it?

And I am angry again.

Ten.
She was told I'd be taken away.
She hugged me and said
'Be brave and try and see the nasty man.'
And so I am scared
But feel I need to be brave for her

You smile and we picnic
Tuna and mayo- my favourite
You bring out a kite and I watch it soar
And it is free and I hurt in my stomach
Should I enjoy this? The officer is watching
making notes.

I don't want to speak to him
'You have to, the courts says.'
The video call, I am rude

She is watching and I say everything right
I speak over you
You make a face and I declare
'You're having a bad day.'
To which there are sniggers

I am numb - you are kind
I worry, you come to greet me
But you are kind and smile
I see her glare and I'm a mirror
My stomach churns
You smile

Eleven. At the beach
We laugh at the seagulls
Throw chips and skim pebbles
Free

Video call at night
I am rude- full of loathing
A little voice in the background
'Daddy, look at me!'
Makes me pause - I am not your only world.

I am told
That his child should not be there
Whilst the call takes place - it is my special time
So I echo it back at him
As expected

Thirteen
I lash out
In pain
Home feels safe
The constant twists and turns
Should they feel safe?

With him feels new still
The quiet
The real safety
The acceptance
His other watches me
As I twist and turn his words
She is carefree and in his lap

I thought we were past this
He frowns when I try to push
All the right buttons
But instead he shakes his head
And stays quiet

I am dropped off
To my version of safety
The twists and turns
Years later
In therapy I will realise the words
Manipulation
Malicious mother syndrome

But for now
She is the best
And for her, I declare

'I don't love you.'

Disclaimer for the professionals:

I am not allowed to.

Alien - an estranged father

'I don't love you.'
It feels like an every Saturday ritual.

Family Matters
The posters say.

To the mother maybe.
But only her family
I am not allowed to be classed as such.

My princess refuses to say my name
She stutters over 'Daddy.'
Soils before seeing me

I am alien to her
She scratches, kicks, spits
The aggression, sickening
Somehow it feels deserved.

For not bearing the unbearable
Not allowed to be father in the marriage
Did I think it would change after
I became alien
Smiling, eating, everything, hurt.

Fast forward
Family Courts
The officer smiles
I trust, stupidly
Naive

And then they say
I can pay to see my daughter
Every Saturday
Supervised

Like a criminal
As if I need to be checked
In a clinical room
With superficial happy rainbows

She kicks and screams
The officer sends the case for review
The mother plays the part so well
'I'm trying but she doesn't like you.'

The innocence and false narrative
Is lost on the courts
Who send it back for review
Every Saturday
With gifts sent in between

Indirect contact they call it
So what have I got now?

I want to scream
But I am alien

Call the police
My daughter says
When she sits opposite me
And the Psychologist watches her carefully
Ordered by the courts
Eight years too late

Effects of parental alienation
Emotional abuse of child
By resident parent
Should be music to my ears
At last

But it has just begun
The alien is rude to me
I am not her father
Every statement of love
Is met with cold indifference

And her primary caregiver
Pulls the strings
So during moments of natural happiness
When my princess flits back
The alien comes back

I love you
I say when she's angry
I love you
I say when she's rude
I love you
Is my mantra through the icy toxic
uncompromising
Behaviour

I am spied on
Reports are made
Via the alien
Fed back to the mothership
And yet I continue

In the hope she knows
That once upon a time
I held her
And melted
And she was as pure as the first snow
And I was her world

If ever you should tread in my shoes
Father, mother, child
It is a lonely road
And so keep living
Even when you hit crossroads

So when the world you made yours

Crumbles
You are not solitary
You are caught when you
Fall

'Daddy,' my other world
Pure and untouched wraps her
Soft pudge around me
And I wish it was the same
For the alien I try to remember

But is continuing to become a fuzzy memory

Stay strong
They say
'Father must stay patient.'
The professionals say
As if I am responsible
For the alien
When I cannot even be me in her presence

Insults come
Double digits now
Softness replaces the angles
But the eyes remain unforgiving

I'm sorry I left you
Remains unsaid
Years to come

I will see her
Unprotected against the emotional
Rollercoaster

Her primary caregivers
Unrelenting punishment for me.

Disclaimer for all involved:
No winners or winnings for this journey.

Copper (On social anxiety)

Wake up
Copper rolls in my mouth

Routine
Tick, tick, tick
Seconds pass
Tick, tick, tick
It is time
Copper rolls in my mouth

The bus is late
Copper rolls in my mouth

The bus is full
Copper rolls in my mouth

I forget the change
Copper rolls in my mouth

The bus goes black
Copper rolls in my mouth

I step off the bus
Everything loud
Breathing, laughing, stepping, running

Copper rolls in my mouth

I sit in class
Easy A
Copper rolls in my mouth

I eat, alone
With friends
Copper rolls in my mouth

Cup is empty
Bus back home
Copper rolls in my mouth

I go home to my safe four walls
And drink the copper away
Breath
Anchor
Acid in my stomach
Subsides

You are safe
Copper tries
You are confident
Copper struggles
Too hard

I am a sandwich in bed
Between weighted blanket and

Mattress
Too hard

Tomorrow, we try
The too hard again.

Breaking Chains

It was the last straw
He said and so I found myself
Alone in a room
With someone who could help

She had been gentle on the phone
Understanding, and it made my heart splinter
That someone could understand
That like an addict
I needed the harsh and chaos

The high of love
And the low of love
The sweet of love
And the sour of love
The ease of love
And the pain of love

But he had shook his head
This isn't me
The knife and fear crippled me
Betrayed
A year of giving him my everything
And he calls me chaos

Chaos? I had spat
My face wet and hot
But my blood was cold
My feet frozen
He wouldn't

And so I sat with someone
Who could help
Will he come back?
I am hopeful
And she glimpses the child in me

We don't focus on the outcome
She is direct but soft
Let's work on you

Me- but I'm good
So what if I had
Called him repeatedly
Suspected him of cheating
Screamed at him
And I'd only hit him once
Maybe twice

It's normal

And that's where we began
Why was it normal?
And why did I crave it?

I am five and scared
They're fighting
Dishes flying
Spaghetti on the fridge door

Crying
Hug my blanket
Present me holds her
Reassures her she is not to blame
This is not your normal

Pinch- come back.
My face is wet
My heart is raw
Throat aches

I discover it was not normal

To feel unsafe is not normal
To want to test
To see if they will stay in chaos
Is not normal
To push and manipulate
Not normal

I am seven
Hungry at school
I cannot eat
Mum had thrown my things together

We're leaving

But when I go home
They are cuddling on the sofa
My things are packed
We're staying love
Kisses and laughs

I push away the memory
In a compartment
But present me opens it
This is not normal
You deserve to feel secure

Open my eyes
Wet
Heart, raw
Throat, aches
Chest, heavy

Did he make you feel safe?
Yes
Did it scare you?
And a chink
In my chaotic armour

She knows me
Understands

It is not easy
Breaking chains
Of a childhood
That was not hazy happiness

But a high low
Of bittersweet closeness
Of promised ride or dies
Of unspoken rules
That we don't talk about
What happened last night
At school

Snap
A mother wound unclasps from my heart
Clunk
A father chain falls to the ground
Thud
My heart thumps
Scared, new and anxious

Who am I without
The hold of the past
Without this addiction of chaos
What do I hold onto?

Distant whisper
Of my five year old
Waving

Safety
Peace
Love

It can be had. seven year old me says
And teenage me
Shrugs
Pretty without her sulk
And my present me agrees

I am loved
I am safe
I release all that hurt me
And move safely into my new space
Of love and healthy
Attachment

My new way of thinking
Is hard to maintain
It spills over
High and low of healing
The chains that kept me
Bound to old patterns
But then I am aware

And change happens

I am loved.
Eventually.

Suitcase

It has been heavy for sometime
Unnoticed at first
Numb and raw
Scared and new
But then it was packed
Visited by few
The house, is just that, without you.

The days become weeks
And the weight is there but unaware still
Like overripe fruit not yet spoilt
The smell just about lingering
Of grief not quite processed
In the flurry of wills yet to read
And wealth and affairs to be rectified

And bills to be paid
And corners to be cleaned
And beds to be washed
And people to be seen

Empty containers
In the bin
I cannot care for recycling
For saving the world

Cannot be reached
When mine has been buried

Cold
Alone
No busy-ness to mislead
Me, into thinking all is level
Heart ache, is packed
Into the corner of a vent

Rooms echo
Night is loud
Day is quiet
And grief is packed
Into my stomach

Heavy but not hungry
The food goes cold
Binned and overflowing
Waste
Weighs the disposal men
As they carry the coloured vessels from the
house
That remain, just that, without you

Heavy now to wake up
Eyes not rested cannot open
Bones protest
Blanket wrapped

Sadness is cold
In the house
That stays, just that, without you.

Counterfeit talk
Idles by me
As I stare ahead
Outside of the house
The window leaks a world
Too much to comprehend
Without you

Memories now packed
In my head weighing me down
Hurting to put down
Aching to carry
Shoulders now slouched
From the unpacking that needs doing
But too painful to carry on

Lead legs
My thoughts are merciless
As I try to walk
To drink
To a parched closed up tongue
But instead we stay
Immobile in our grief

Too heavy to unpack
This suitcase
You left behind
Me
In the house, that stays as just that
Without you

Help from the concerned
Professional intervention

She says my grief is weighing me down
Even though I have lost
So much of my layers
A cardigan, a coat, a scarf
Make the volume needed
So there is no medical concern|
For those that see me a number
In a house
That remains
Just that
Without you

A suitcase
I carry
Everyday
For you are a home
Within me
That cannot be taken
To a house

That stays
Without you
Just that.

Listen to me

Morning and the day seems empty
Staring at my phone
And not my to do list

Listen to me

Must move quicker
According to people in charge
Little people in charge
Oblivious to my busy blank head

Listen to me

Playground etiquette
Abandons me
As the noise fills my mind
Everything loud and quiet at once
Like an exam
In the middle of a market

Listen to me

'Love you, have a nice day.'
Do they hear
That I am not there

But in another country
Maybe

Listen to me

Working constantly
With too many tabs open
Waiting for the focus to come
And in between
I eat
Sporadically
Good and bad

Listen to me

Laundry done
But then a sock retrieved
And a dusty floor noticed
Half a bucket full
Phone ringing
Too many tabs open

Listen to me

Desperate
Rushing
Heart racing
World is loud
Hungry

Cold
Now hot

Listen to me

Deadline met
But only just
Outperformed by none
But only just
Brilliant, creative
And made just in time
 Listen to me

In this electronic environment
The faulty gene
Wakes up
Cortisol triggered
Train is lost
Thought gone
Everyone is normal
Happy bubbles!

I scream
Listen!

Me too!

Gone: Grief through the eyes of an autistic young adult

During lockdown
Dad realised
How special I was
When Mum had done it all
But now she's gone

I don't want to sit
And learn good
I want to sleep
Under my heavy blanket
On my clean mattress
In my tidy room
And feel good

But she's gone

Dad tries everything
But Mum used to
Know everything he is trying
He is not good at it
He needs her to show it
But she's gone

There should be a book
I hear him
He is sad
And tired
Grey around the brown

Not blue like mine
Like mum's
But it's good mine are blue
Like mum's
Because she's gone

Therapy
Is suggested
And Dad is desperate
He puts me in a room
Clean and white
With a chair hard

And a blanket not as heavy
But still feels nice
Like mum

No eye contact
Doesn't speak
No college right now

Therapy is nice and simple
No looking

And a blanket
Quiet from the house
Because she's gone

How do you feel?
I hurt here,
My chest
Is not soft no more

When she was going
She held me
And said with warm on my cheek
'You are growing and changing
And I can't wait to meet you
Again.'

But she's gone

Therapy smiles
'She meant Heaven.'
And it feels good
The pain goes a bit
So I smile
No looking

No looking she reassures me
Where is the pain now?
Second therapy
A little in my chest

Shall we discuss Heaven?
Where Mum is waiting
I tell her it seems good
Peaceful
Mum is drinking
Her favourite
White coffee, sweet

How did Mum make you feel?
Safe, I say loudly
Not looking
But still looking
Therapy is smiling

And teaches me
To hold myself
When I want to remember Mum
Who is gone

Therapy says
It is havening
To make me feel safe
Because my safe is gone
I tell her
Haven
Is Heaven
Without the E
Like M and E

Like Mum
Therapy says

And I say
She's gone
Without ME

And now I see red
And feel the pain strong
In my chest
In my fingers

Not looking
But the sound is loud
Therapy asks me
To hold me
To Haven without the E
And see what Mum is doing
Drinking coffee

In green gardens
And the pain goes
And I am at college
Not looking
But working
Doing good

So when I see Mum
Because she's gone

She can touch my even hard chest
That doesn't hurt as much
And say
You've changed and grown
Since I've been gone

And I hold me
Saying it's Mum
Because she has gone
Without me.

My body talks

I stopped telling
The professionals
What hurt and where
So they stopped giving the why

Instead I started to listen
My head said
I thought too much
Of things that didn't need my attention

And my jaw informed me
Stiffly
That I constantly tightened it
To stop saying
What it really wanted

My shoulders said
I carried the weight
Of things others should have carried

And my fingers said
I had held onto
Things that had to
Be released

My knees clicked
To let me know
A change of direction was needed

And my feet ached
To let me know
The same
That if I didn't
I would feel stuck

And so I stopped popping
The blister packs
And started listening
When I stopped talking

And now my body has been quiet for some time
Letting my heart and mouth
Do the talking

But all inside
Are lit with
White flags
So now that I'm finally listening
When my body talks
It no longer needs to shout red
And I am not the bull.

Inner Child

I sat with my six year old
And told her it's not her fault
She didn't want to talk at first
So I held her instead

I sat with my 9 year old
And we linked little fingers
Hers so soft
And she said
'Don't cry, I love you.'
Was it my voice or hers?

I visited my twelve year old
Awkward, clumsy, unsure
And told her
She was perfect
She didn't need to fit into
The box everyone kept trying to put her in

I sat long enough with my
Angry sixteen year old
To know that she was not
As she heard daily
Lazy, angry and dumb
But she was grieving

Her life not lived
Whilst everyone was so mobile
And she was frozen

I walked with my twenty year old
To know she was envious
Trying so hard
To please
So I told her to do one thing
She loved everyday

I sat with my burnt out
Thirty year old
Overstimulated and under-loved
And held her hand
Long enough
For her to
Not feel alone

 And today
I sat with present me
And got
All the versions of me
To sit and comfort me

I'm sorry
I love you
Please forgive me
Thank you

And little by little
The layers left
The resistance crumbled
And faith found
A small silver lining on the
Inside
And continued to grow
Until I lit up

Like my inner child
Before the world shaped her.

Healing

The war is over so why do I ready myself for
battle?
The slightest comment or disturbance to the
daily
Rises my hackles and shackles
Why do I keep my weapon of choice ready?
Be it a slice of tongue or an arrow with my
fingers
Why do my eyes flash at other people's fights?
Why do my shoulders feel the weight of the
world?
My storm has passed
Yet it rages inside me
The triggers of lightning crack my memory
Until I no longer am at peace
The hardship has passed
So why am I not at ease?
What am I chasing?
When rainbows are around me?
Who am I trying for? When all that should be
pleased
Is inside me?
The past wars are just that
Past
A dusty date

A hazy fog
Yet the sharp focus of pain
Is a camera lens on my heart
A copper climbing my mouth

The war is over, so why am I still fighting?
When really, the past is a thread to cut
The future is a stitch to unravel
The present is a broken piece to fix

And what I am fighting no longer exists
It is a feeling that long should have past
But we hold onto it
it's a part of us
And without it
The copper climbs into our hearts and minds
We venture into
Unknown worlds
Without the war
That has long been over

The real fight
Is a fight to train
The body
For the new battle
For peace

The tools are rusty
Unused

46

Awkward and testing
Trialling and erring
Trying and striving
Often tiring and resting

Put down your weapons and give
Attention to the tools
Of new thoughts and words
New hope and energy
Breath in fresh air
Of time and space
Of one and wholeness.

Do not destruct
What is already broken
But fix
What is felt now. Be one
Be whole
Just be
Today.

Mountains & Fences

I built a picket
A small one
To show my values
Were to be respected

You trampled and
Sat
On what was left
An occupied territory on my broken
barrier

I built a bigger fence
Solid wood
Great foundations
Cemented six foot in the soil

You rocked the foundation
As you pillaged it down
Splinters cracked
At my lines
That spelt the
Respect
You did not give

I made an iron fist
Unmoveable
Unshakeable
You bumped fist
As a friend
My 'No!'
Became your foe
Before I knew it
The iron was foil
Open, crinkly and wrapped
Around your finger

I built a mountain
Hurting from the breaches
You tried
You climbed
You fell
I did not waver
I did not splinter
My heart is there
Unattainable

Too bad
You were heedless
And now my broken pieces
Are whole boundaries
And must be heeded.

This shoe hurts

I tried to wear a shoe
And it didn't quite fit
It was too stiff, too proper
With no room to grow

I wore something someone said
Was elegant and not meant
For someone like me
My heritage
My colonised country
Were not quite
The right fit for something
So refined

I wore a trainer
That had a stiff and unforgiving leather tongue
As I walked
The top of my foot protested
Not too harsh
It blistered angrily
Enough said

I tried the slipper
Freedom with room to breath
The way my ancestors walked

But it was cold and foreign to me

I sat with different shoes
Ones that restricted me
Ones my feet tried to please
Ones that were too high
And ones that were too low

And each time
I felt inferior
Does this item really belong to me?
And do I really fit into it?

Of all the shoes that I tried on
I found
Judgement
Constriction
And very little empathy
They were not mine
And I was not for them

And so I sat with my feet
Open and naked
Took in the brown skin
So perfectly wrinkly
Protecting me
As I walked the rocky path
And realised
The shoes I was already in

Were perfectly fine
For my journey.

52

Belonging

I have this thought
And it won't go away
Like a shadow
It is my most loyal friend

I don't belong here
It whispers as I sit
With my own
Skin colour

And my mother's savage daughter
Whispers sardonically
'Raised with books
Not with looks.'

And so I find
People of the same faith
But even then there are branches
Hanafi, Shafi, Malaki, Hanbali

And so I sit
With people
Raised with books
But I like deep epic reads
Not the five decades of grey

And so I ask
The savage voice
To be kinder
And stop cursing at me
Breaking down
What I love
And making me feel
Like I'm not enough

And my mother's savage daughter
Whispers
In all her abandonment
That I am just you
You must accept
And grow
And if you want to change my whispers
You need to speak your truth louder

And so I sat
With people of my colour
And found common ground

With people of my faith
I raised my finger
And proclaimed~
One love

And with people of books
I found it was enough

That they read

And more than I was different
I found
That I was more accepting of me
And them
And so
I found an us.

Broken

How loud
The silence is
That exists between people
Who once spoke

How hateful
Is the air
That suffocates those that
Once loved

How strange
Are siblings
That are no longer family

How cold
Are friends
Who once wore bracelets

How broken
Is the husband
Who's wife once waited

How hurt
Is the wife
Who's husband once came home

How worn
Is the toy
The child once played with

How broken
Are the ancient castles
Now replaced
By shiny new
'Homes.'
That we have
'Outgrown.'

Come back to me

I find often
I go back to that day
And the hurt cripples me
Sunny skies
Suddenly bleak

And so I come back
With the self discipline
Of a nil by mouth
Patient

The other day
Whilst shopping
I went back to the day
You left me
Anxiety came where
Certainty had once been

I reaffirmed sternly
To come back
To the now

Amidst hiking
A strenuous mount
I remembered

The joyous pain
Of being new homeowners
With you

Eyes hot
I came back to climbing
And pushed through the burn
Until my mind was focused on just making it to
the top

And often I find myself living
In that wonderful bubble
Safe with you
Your deceit
Your lies
Our twisty turns
Highs and lows
More lows than highs

And in that moment
New me falters
Struggles
And my throat closes
My eyes are hot
Cheeks wet
Chest aches

And then I remember
To breath

One breath to recognise
One breath to process
One to release
And come back to the present
Come back to me.

One day
I will stop
Running from the memories
And one day I will be happy
Being still
Not climbing
Shopping
Working

I will come back to me.

Anchor

Find a safe place

So I close my eyes
What does it feel like?
The air is warm
Like the best chocolate
Melted in a cup
Sliding down my throat
Heating my inner

The ground is forgiving
On the pinks and yellows of my soles
Silky sands
Helping me pad

To comforting waters
That caress me
Blanket me
Secure me

What can you see?
Oh, if only you could join me!
Blues and greens
Golden yellows
Fruits ready for heavenly consumption

And soothing animals

What do I hear, you ask?
All the sounds
That evoke
Endorphins
And seratonins
And make me
Smile

What do I taste?
Sweet cotton candy air

And what do smell?
I breath and the warm sweetness
Is like a bakery
Of fresh comfort

And you say,
Come back to what hurt you

And I do it
In a safe bubble
In a safe place
That is inside of me
And cannot be taken away

My armour against the world.

Talk to me

Tell me your hurt
That won't go away
Like a child who has lost
Their say

Tell me what wakes you
Fearful and breathless.
So we may share
A resolution for rest

Tell me what angers you
You are certain
It cannot be calmed
But from where I sit
Cold grief can be warmed

Tell me of the copper coils
In your mouth and stomach
Of the weight of new
And old
Tell me so I can teach you
How overcoming will help you
Grow

Tell me how the grief

Weighs you down so
I can keep
Bearing your weight with you
So you can hopefully
Sleep

Tell me how you struggle
With the constant pain
Of guilt, hate and shame
Tell me so I can
Make you love you again

Tell me so I can tell it back
On a day when you are kinder
That one day you came in pieces
And session by session
With this sole vessel
We came back
Whole and in peace.

Talk to me today
So you can talk tomorrow
So your children can walk
Lighter
Without paying what ails you
To their own
Talk to me often
So those that suffer
Are few.

Talk to me...

Hungry Ghosts - Addiction

I often wonder
Who I am without
You

I see you want me
You itch and claw
Until I am consumed by you
And you, by me

I go about my day
And when I feel that want
That longing
I am normally
High functioning
Distrusting
Uncomfortable

I sit with a vessel
To understand
You
And she asks
If I was ever lonely

And I am seven
And you are there

Giving me happiness
Where I would normally find none

And I am fourteen
You are giving me acceptance
Where I find none

And I am twenty five
Amidst shame
You love me

And I am thirty
Amidst pain
You hold and comfort me

And so I sit
With my hungry ghosts
That were never connected
And I meet them
And make them meet
And in the realms

My need for you
Softens
Slowly
Painfully
Excruciatingly

A knife

In reverse
It is not easy
Suffocating at times
You ask me if I'm ready

To increase the time between the itch
And decrease the time of self love

And it is breathtakingly
Beautiful and tragic
As I recognise
What you filled
That I now need to

The void left
By my hungry ghosts
Past and present
Needs my care
My love
My attention
My discipline
My kindness
My validation

I am

980 days ghost free.

Lessons from a Vessel

They came in their numbers
I had things to learn
Naive me
Held onto the result

But the journey
Made me
It made me hear
Made me see

A slump stand up straighter
Once the weight of grief left
And a sparkle
To their tone
Where once they sounded bereft

A smile
Where once tears were worn
And movement
Where stiffness
Had been born

I learnt
The gift
Of trust

From them to me
And me to them
And the art of focus
Of hearing
Not what was said
But how

And the words of silence
And the words of differently abled
And the words of pain
And the words of labels

I learnt the
Void of absent parents
And became better with my own
I learnt the power of forgiveness
And so was able to let go

I learnt that anger was
Grief
And grief was so heavy

And that anxiety
Was a child
Who had been attacked
So severely

And that words
Held weight

In gold when used correctly

But when used to hurt
Could twist a knife
Directly

Into your subconscious
Where the thoughts cement in
Where layers are built
And then
One day

You came to me
And we became

Lessons in a Vessel
With lessons
From both ends

We held messages
And spaces
Space in those messages
And each one of you
Is a remembered name.

Thank you.